Quilted Memories

CELEBRATIONS OF LIFE  Mary Lou Weidman

C&T PUBLISHING

Dedication

To the good Lord, family and dear friends that make life worth celebrating.

Thank yous

To the C&T publishing team: Todd Hensley, for having the vision to publish this book; to Jan Grigsby, my editor, for her good attitude, kindness, and knowledge in editing and being a "pie-person"; Joyce Lytle for her positive attitude and sweet spirit from the beginning; Christina Jarumay who captured my whimsical and creative vision in the design of the book; Diane Pedersen who used her eyes to help achieve dazzling button ensemble photos. And to photographers Mark Frey and Sharon Risedorph for their professionalism.

This book would not have been possible without the hard work of many good friends. I therefore wish to thank: My family for the many hours they were ignored while I "put in a couple more stitches" or "typed just one more sentence."
Julie Lynch for her wonderful appliqué, friendship, pattern help, and creative input.
Naomi Ishiguro for her fabulous piecing skill on borders, positive ways and wonderful humor when the going was tough.
Pam Clarke for her creative one-of-a-kind machine quilting:
Pam quilted her magic in every quilt of mine seen in this book.
My mother, Geneva Donahue, for sewing down the binding of many quilts for me.
Dad, Ted Donahue, for cheering Mom on.
Aunt Lu and Marion Morrison for being the best cheerleaders anyone could ever ask for.
Nancy Nelson for her knowledge, word processing skills, and cheerful attitude in typing and transferring this to disk for the editor. Lorie Latta for her intelligence and know-how on my manuscript. Rik Nelson and his family for the use of the picnic ribbon on page 5. And last, but certainly not least, the students who participated in my Holiday Harry challenge, and the many students who offered their work and their questions to help me with the content of this book. The people I meet in workshops make this business so very worthwhile.

Cover quilt story:

SAILING INTO SPRING 60" X 73"

I am an avid gardener when I can find time and so is my husband. Our yard is a sanctuary for both of us and our kids have happy memories spent playing back there. I wanted to do a garden-type quilt with all of us but did not want the usual backyard scene. After my friend Naomi pieced a border for me, I looked at it and thought about a ship. On the ship are my husband and I gardening. In the portholes are my three kids. My son-in-law often comments that I forgot to put him in. So, if you will notice behind the tree is a figure peeking out...it's Mark, my son-in-law. We actually get along great but he is a lot of fun to tease. I should mention too that I worked on this at a retreat and my friends Sally and Tonye laughed and said, "You should call it Sailing into Spring." Sally's mom looked at the quilt and said, "A ship with a garden?" Maybe it's just me, but I thought it was a terrific idea. My kids like it too.

Copyright 2001 Mary Lou Weidman

Editor: Jan Grigsby
Technical Editor: Joyce Engels Lytle
Copy Editor: Stacy Chamness
Cover Designer: Christina D. Jarumay
Design Director/Book Designer: Christina D. Jarumay
Production Assistant: Kirstie L. McCormick
Graphic Illustrations: Tim Manibusan
Front cover photo: Sharon Risedorph, Author photo: Dennis Stanciu, How-to photos and buttons Steven Buckley, Photographic Reflections, styled by Diane Pedersen. Photos on the following pages Sharon Risedorph 12, 14, 18, 21, 24, 25, 27, 30, 31, 33, 36, 37, 43, 45, 49, 51, 56, 61, 79 and 87. All other quilt photos Mark Frey.

Attention Teachers:
C&T Publishing, Inc. encourages you to use this book as a text for teaching. Contact us at 800-284-1114 or www.ctpub.com for more information about the C&T Teachers Program.

Library of Congress Cataloging-in-Publication Data
Weidman, Mary Lou,
  Quilted memories : celebrations of life / Mary Lou Weidman.
      p. cm.
Includes index.
  ISBN 1-57120-166-1 (paper trade)
  1. Appliqué–Patterns. 2. Quilts–Design. 3. Quilts–Themes, motives. I. Title.
  TT779 .W45 2001
  746.46'041–dc21
                                        2001001986

Published by C&T Publishing, Inc.
P.O. Box 1456
Lafayette, California 94549

Printed in the USA
10 9 8 7 6 5 4 3 2 1

Introduction

I thought about the many ways I could begin this book. Since this subject is so special to me I wanted to move you, the reader, to be excited, tearful, sentimental, and happy with the ideas and design opportunities awaiting you with celebration quilts. Beyond the design, bright color, embellishments, and techniques that make up these celebration quilts, is a sentimental journey. To help you "see" what I am trying to convey, I created a little story for you to read.

One day your doorbell rings. You open the door and see the parcel carrier looking back at you as he hands you a rather large box. After thanking the carrier you bring the box inside and discover it is from your mother's cousin.

You remember your mother's cousin as a fun person. One weekend many years ago comes to mind, as you recall a special picnic at the lake that included many family members. A clear blue sky, beautiful blue water, and the smells of fresh air and barbecue bring the memories of that experience back to you. Cousin Bob brought his canoe and your Aunt Lisa brought her favorite chocolate cake. Uncle Red and the other men folk took turns turning the crank for homemade ice cream. A cousin you barely remember sat on a bee that day and ran into the lake, clothes and all. In the evening, relatives gathered by the fire to sing songs and roast marshmallows.

All these memories rushed to your thoughts just by reading your cousin's name on the parcel. What fun you thought, as you reminisced.

You tear the box open to find a note: "Dear _____, I am a friend of your mother's cousin _____, and she asked me that if anything happened to her, to send this to you. She wanted someone in the family to have this quilt as it might have special meaning to them. She hoped you would love and appreciate this special piece of your family's history. Sincerely, _____"

As you open the quilt, you are delighted to see what appears to be a story of sorts. Pictured is the picnic celebration at the lake you remembered with fondness. Your mother's cousin's cabin appears in calico and polka dots. Children are playing in bathing suits by the lake,

and the name of each child is neatly stitched above each figure. Your mother's cousin's husband is holding a toy boat. There by the cabin is your mother's cousin holding a chocolate-colored cake. A flag flies high over the top of the figures. On the bottom of the quilt is an actual blue ribbon. "Liberty Lake Picnic—1935" it announces.

Family buttons, a lodge pin, and pieces of an old flag are all included. Details like a pail and shovel, birds, a sand castle, a row boat, fishing poles and bait, dragonflies, and kites flying make this quilt fun to look at. "This is a piece of history," you tell yourself, "all of it is preserved in a wonderful quilt to be shared with others." As you gathered the quilt in your arms, you felt like you were receiving a hug from an old aunt.

Now, the point of this story is, how many quilts do you see that were made showing day-to-day life in 1935? And how many quilts have you seen with the names of family members, the things they liked to do, the places they worked, or the activities from their day-to-day lives? How many old quilts have you seen with sentiments, stories of holidays and celebrations, truisms, or Bible verses? Eighty years from now what will people know about you and how you celebrated life? Will they know about picnics on the beach, your special pie recipe, a friendship, a grandbaby, the Fourth of July, Valentine's dinners, Halloween pranks, Easter egg hunts, Hanukkah family celebrations, green soda bread, walks in the garden, baking cookies with children, the smell of the first spring flowers? Will anyone know who your special friends were? How many things have you written down or recorded in a quilt? How many vacations have you taken that could be journaled in quilt form?

Telling stories is what this book is about. Telling your story: who and what you love, and how you celebrate life, and then getting it onto cloth to be enjoyed, researched, held, fondled, and more important, cherished, for many years to come. Remembering what happened to you today—next week and this year will change as time marches on. These quilts become journal pieces in fabric and become a legacy of celebrations to be shared by those people who are privileged to view them.

Contents

A Bit of Background: Questions Most Asked

44" X 58"

My grandmother actually taught me my first quilt stitches, then in the 1970s I started quilting as a hobby. I had a background as a painter and generally liked to try my hand at anything that encouraged my artist. I thought quilting would be a short-lived hobby.

I like people. Because of my interest in people, I like to hear about what makes people happy. It seemed fairly clear one day that I should keep quilting and include things about people. My focus changed, and I no longer thought of quilts as something to cover my beds. I gave myself permission to experiment and not worry about wasting fabrics. I realized that mistakes were good opportunities for knowledge.

I have been asked how I come up with all of the ideas for my quilts. For me, it has been simple. I listen and watch people. I like to record what makes people different from one another, and what makes them want to celebrate simple things as well as traditional things.

Do you think it is a waste of time to sit on a chair in your backyard and enjoy the sights and smells? Do you allow yourself a chance to sit and enjoy the sun or a breeze? How about taking time to listen? Your senses are for your enjoyment and are your best tools for ideas and creativity.

People say to me that they like my quilts because they are fun, bright, and most importantly, happy. I can't tell you the number of people that compliment me by saying, "Your quilts always make me smile." As quilt lovers, we want to see happy, positive images in quilts. If you, like many of us, have had something sad or tragic in your life, please take the positive approach to designing what you see. This world needs more happiness and certainly more laughter. I can promise you that if you follow this one rule, you will have many more viewers who will be glad to see, walk up, and enjoy your quilt.

I also have people ask how I handle a quilt that isn't turning out, or how I handle discouragement. Many times you need to get away from the project and put it away for another day. And as for getting discouraged, I really don't think a quilt is enough to garner the energy of discouragement. It's only fabric. If I ever get really discouraged over a quilt, it goes to the rummage sale and I forget about it and start another one. The process is more important than the quilt: It's what you learned and how you developed that is important.

Right Brain vs. Left Brain, or How'd You Think of That?

I teach a lot of workshops, and it used to surprise me when someone would walk into the room and say, "I have been scared to death to take this class." I couldn't understand why a class in which a person would be encouraged to use their imagination would intimidate anyone, because essentially it is so much fun. I now know after many such encounters that it is intimidating and scary for people to design their own pictures, and later, quilts. This puts them in a position for other people to criticize and say, "What in the world is this quilt about?" "What the heck were you thinking?" "Is that a rabbit or a dancing horse?"

And actually from my point of view this is ok. How many times do you go to a quilt show, walk down the aisle, and never break stride? I see people doing this all the time. Many times a glance is all your eyes need to see the whole story when it comes to a quilt. You see the block pattern, the color, and the borders. No need to slow down. But if you see a quilt with people or animals or a neighborhood or a vase filled with interesting things, then this is reason enough for a viewer to break stride and take time to "see" what is included in your quilt. Putting a story into a quilt about a celebration invites the viewer to share the memory.

I have read everything I could find about creativity over my lifetime. I have also read a lot about writing and what is called writer's block. Writer's block is similar to what many quilters go through when they start having doubts about their design.

Whether you know it or not, this is the battle of right brain vs. left brain. Both sides of the brain have their own roles. Left brain is in charge of analytical traits, reasoning, and math. Right brain likes play, design, and creativity. Now, we need both our right brain and our left brain, but there is something you may not know. The left brain likes to take over in some people, and in others the right brain takes over. When you go to work on a quilt design and you start thinking "I can't do this! What made me think I can design my own quilt?" that is the left brain saying, "Hey, let me take over, let's do something I like to do." Many people follow the left brain and give up. But if you can challenge your brain and give it a few right-brain exercises, you can get into right-brain mode.

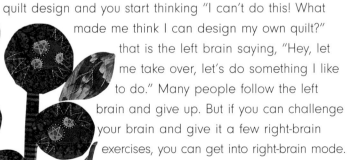

GOOD ADVICE QUILT 60" X 56"

I like the idea of putting inspirational things into some of my quilts. It makes sense that one day when you are no longer in the world, your quilt could still bless people with something wise you shared. "Good thoughts bare good fruit, and man is his own gardener" is an old adage that proves true today.

Quilted Memories

Being a Cheerleader

You may have never been a cheerleader in past years, but this is a good chance to become one. Over the years I have met some wonderful artists, including both quilters and others who work in paints and other mediums. I made a very important observation. Many students get a degree in art and have all the talent in the world, but don't have the confidence to follow through. Often, after they graduate, they slow down their painting process and go into another field altogether. I believe firmly that this is because they "need" to hear and internalize someone saying, "You are so talented", "I love your work", "You have such good insight", "You have such a good style", "Your designs are so original," and so on. Without someone telling them, they fall back into not working and producing. Many give up completely. Why? Because they lack a cheerleader.

This is why I stress that if you are going to be a good artist (quilt designer), you must be your own best cheerleader. A good cheerleader rises above criticism or ridicule. They actually produce more and are more content with what they do. They can stretch because they enjoy the process and the product.

This is what I want you to do for yourself: Tell yourself you are doing well, your quilt is going to be great, your colors make you smile, and that your shapes are pleasing. Laugh, pat yourself on the back, be amused at your ideas, etc. There is always room to use a discerning eye and say, "I need to change that," but always be positive and kind with yourself. You will reap the rewards of your positive input. It's not always as important for the acceptance of others as it is for the acceptance of yourself. You are often your own harshest critic.

Keeping a Notebook

I often tell my students to take a piece of paper, pick a theme, and challenge themselves to write thirty things that relate to the theme they selected. You may not need thirty, but you've put your mind in a creative mode by challenging it. The other interesting thing that the list exercise does remind your brain to be on the lookout for things that might relate to that theme. I tell students that in the next few weeks they will be coming up with ideas, even though the exercise might be over.

The secret to right brain vs. left brain is to say "Nothing is too silly to try," or at least to give yourself permission to stretch and not worry what someone else thinks.

Creating an Atmosphere
of Creativity

AUNTS!!! 67" X 73"

I remember times I spent with my three aunts—May, Bess, and Rose—in South Dakota. Celebrations of any kind always included good home cooking. People on my dad's side of the family took their pies seriously, and were all good cooks. I thought it would be fun to portray them all with parts of a pie. I remember them with aprons and clothes that fit a certain time period. My grandmother used to tell me any woman who wanted to keep her husband should get up two hours ahead and fix herself up and have a hot breakfast or she'd lose him to the lady down the street. All of my aunts always fixed themselves up...Grandma, too (I hope my husband doesn't read this!).

I would be remiss if I did not address one of the most important, yet most overlooked, elements of creativity. I often like to point out to students that I have noticed that the people we are around influence our work. Negative people stifle creativity.

In a flower garden, you have roses, orchids, lilies, and other flowers. These flowers would represent the wonderful, nurturing, and positive people in your life. You are influenced, fed, and encouraged by these lovely flowers (people).

On the other hand, all flower gardens have dandelions, crab grass, and weeds that choke out the flowers, and suck all the moisture, energy, and vitamins right out of the good plants. These weeds take valuable time to deal with. The more time you deal with weeds, the less time you have to deal with the beautiful flowers that nurture you and your creative side.

I did a little weeding in my garden when I realized that I had people who were taking my creative energy away with comments and actions that weren't positive. It is good to think about the good and not-so-good side of people that you are around. On the other hand you can't be so sensitive that even your roses can't say, "Gee, Mary Lou, that dog would have looked better if you hadn't cut that fourth leg off." I actually did have someone say that to me one day, and she is still a rose

in my friendship flower garden. I tried not to be hurt that she didn't like my three-legged dog. A weed might say something like, "Honey, you haven't made a decent quilt since you started quilting, so give it up." Or, "You call that appliqué?, I call it basting!" Do you see the difference?

To be creative, we want people who can tell us that they like what we do because they can see we are happy doing it. If we are lucky, they can give us a little positive criticism. But you don't want to listen to someone who does not understand story quilts and does not want to. You want someone to say, "Hey, why not put your favorite cousin in there?" "Why not put a purple cow in that field?" "Put a bee on that man's nose." It's fun when your best flowers (friends or family) come up with creative ideas that make them feel like they are a part of your quilt.

So, the point of my going into this is; surround yourself with happy, positive people who are going to nurture your ideas and you. They don't need to see your vision, but they should stand by you while you work to support what your mind's eye perceives. Work on seeing what's good with life. Make a difference by being a positive person.

15

You, Too, Can Draw

HAPPY THINGS QUILT 28" X 52"

When my children were small we had a guessing game that we all loved to play. I would take a piece of paper, and as I drew the kids would guess what I was drawing. I had to constantly think of new things to draw so the game would remain a challenge for them. I thought that things in a child's room would be an excellent quilt to make. I sat down and thought about some of the things I had drawn and got my fabrics and scissors out, and this quilt is the result. This would make an excellent quilt to hang in a child's room or at Grandmother's house for a game that could be played together to create a wonderful memory.

After teaching workshops for a number of years, if I have learned one thing it's that quilters are afraid to draw. Actually, I would say most of the population is afraid of drawing. Many students look at me on the way into class and feel they need to declare, "I am not an artist!" or "I never could draw!" or "I am taking this class but don't expect me to draw anything!" and similar proclamations.

This used to bother me, but not any more. I have learned a secret: With a little encouragement and coaxing, anyone can draw. I can honestly say that I haven't had a student yet who was hopeless. Even my husband drew himself watering the garden after I gave him a short lesson in drawing. My kids laughed and were delighted when they saw the drawing because it looked just like him (cartoon style).

"Easy does it" is a good statement to keep in mind while drawing. Get yourself a good eraser, a sharp pencil or two, and give yourself some time. Many times students think they need to shade and fill in texture, etc. For my type of quilts you need simple shapes with clean lines. Spare the detail and let your fabric do the work. For example, a house is a square, a window in the house is a square, and the door is a rectangle. A chimney is a rectangle and the smoke coming out of the chimney could be buttons. A tree is a circle with a rectangle for a trunk. You can design anything using shapes. The only downside to this that I can think of, is time. Many impatient quilters will say to me, "I don't have time to figure this out, can you draw me a quick clock?" You do have time. We live in a hurry-hurry world. Slow down, take some time, and teach yourself how many things are simple shapes. A person's head is a circle, the trunk of the body is an oval of sorts, arms are two rectangles and so are legs. Then the fun begins and you can dress your person.

I suggest you start by looking at people and things with shapes in mind. For example, a teapot for example is a circle with a base. The handle is an oval and the spout is a rounded rectangle. By drawing it over and over on a piece of paper, you can get an assortment of interesting and fun teapots for a wallhanging for a tea lover in your life.

I am always analyzing and noticing shape. I look at people's profiles and noses when I am sitting on an airplane. I often think when I see certain characters that if I portrayed them in a quilt, everyone would laugh and think I made them up. I see some very unusual and colorful people and you will too if you take time to notice. Taking time is the secret. Perhaps you are hurrying and missing many things that you would enjoy if you took some time.

I remember that when I was small my mother would make a point of taking me to visit neighbors to see their gardens. We would stroll down the street and visit in the backyards of people who became friends. Now, I don't think many people take the time to meet their neighbors or enjoy other people's yards. It seems a real shame to me. We are missing so many beautiful moments and things.

So, to summarize; sharp pencils, a good eraser, time, patience, time, practice, time. Guaranteed to produce great results.

PLAID FOLK ART SAMPLER 57" X 52"

I like fabrics and color on black. I started this quilt for a design workshop I teach. I decided to do shapes of that are folksy and things that I like. I thought it needed a stronger border than the diffused color that plaids provide so I used a cheddar fabric to show off the color used in the rest of the quilt. Buttons provided a little more whimsy and fun.

SMILE AND THE WORLD SMILES, TOO 56" X 48"

Sometimes coming home with colorful fabrics after an afternoon of shopping and being with good friends is enough to provide a fun idea for a quilt. I started making a colorful border out of weird Log Cabin blocks and thought about what I wanted for a theme. I decided that it would be fun to do a folk-style wallhanging with a happy theme. I free-form cut my horse and bird and stitched rows of red and white stripes together to make a great flag. Buttons always seem to help add personality. My cousin Lance, whom I consider to be on the serious side, asked if he could have this quilt. It tickles me that he would even want it. I guess it's hard to find a serious quilt in my collection.

Many years ago, I took paper and experimented with cutting out folk-style animals, people, and letters. This takes a little practice but anyone can do it with little difficulty, some patience, and a "can-do" attitude.

There are two approaches to this. One is to draw what you want free-form on a piece of paper. Place that paper in front of you, and as you study the drawing you will cut out your shape. I find that this results in clearer lines and a more predictable product. I've discovered that most quilters like things that are predictable and therfore more controlled. I tell my students to practice on paper and then grab a chunk of fabric and go for it.

My favorite way to work follows a slightly different approach. I like a quiet place, a chunk of fabric in my hand, some great music in the background, and time to visualize. The idea is to take the fabric in hand, clearly visualize something and then start slowly cutting. When I finish, I am delighted to see that a leg might be shorter than it would have been had I drawn it, or it may be bent in a fun, whimsical position. I like this unplanned, more adventurous approach. I learned a lot of tight, controlled art techniques in school, and it has taken me a long time to set those aside for the sake of making my work more personal.

So, if you would like to try something fun, pick up your scissors and practice some shapes. After you have practiced with paper, take some fabric and try the real thing. You will love this and it will become habit. A hat cut out using this method is surely more interesting than one that is drawn and then cut out perfectly.

Sometimes, the predictable can be perfectly boring. There is a great quilt waiting for you to design, and this method might be one you want to explore. If nothing else, it can give you some good chuckles to see what your hand cuts out.

How to Increase Your
Creativity Quotient

GIVE THANKS YOU'RE NOT A TURKEY 56" X 49"

Thanksgiving is a wonderful time. I teach a lot of workshops based on the idea of Thanksgiving and being thankful on a daily basis. I know that this concept is what makes life joyful. With Thanksgiving as a theme, I cut out a turkey on a trip to Calgary, Alberta, to visit my daughter. I really didn't know what else would be in the quilt until later. I cut out the letters free-form as I wanted a really folksy, whimsical look to go along with the title of the quilt.

1 **Be thankful** for what you have, no matter how simple—clean water, hands to sew, a smile from someone, the smell of strawberries or fresh bread baking, the scent of flowers, a piece of good chocolate, etc. Make a list often to remind yourself of the things you might have taken for granted. Have a contest with yourself and make a list of twenty-five things. Increase it weekly.

2 **Listen** to others. Really, really listen. Listen to how people say things, how they laugh, how they relate. Make it a point to really listen to how a story is being told or what wonderful visual adjectives are being said. If you listen closely, often you can actually "see" with your mind's eye a scene from the story being told. Translate that onto your quilt surfaces. When a friend tells you a story, relax and enjoy it. You might be surprised what kinds of things you hear that could help you to be more creative.

3 **Surround yourself with positive people.** There is nothing more inspiring than a good friend or a wise person who has a positive outlook. When I turned fifty I decided I would keep an eye out for wise women. Wise women are people who are older than you are (generally) and have wisdom that they don't shove at you. They share their wisdom if you are willing to take time and listen.

4 **Take note of what you have in your fabric inventory.** Now take those fabrics and re-stack them by color or by design. If you have always stacked your fabrics by color, perhaps now is the time to re-stack them by polka dots, stripes, stars, or cats. Changing your routine is a good tip for being creative in a new way and shaking things up.

And another note of advice from one who knows: Use your favorite fabrics before they are dated and you don't like them any longer. If you are like me, sometimes you can't cut into your favorite pieces. Years later, you ask yourself what you ever liked about this ugly stuff. (I use these pieces for backing, by the way.)

5 **Play music.** Music has inspired many masters in the art world. Perhaps you have always listened to the same radio station. Why not try to stretch and perhaps pump up the beat. Or maybe you need something very airy and beautiful to inspire you. If you haven't tried music to change your creativity quotient, you are in for a real treat. Ask other quilters what kinds of music they like to listen to. Be open to their choices as well as yours. There is no "right" music. You may find a new song or type of music that sends you on a whole new path of creativity.

6 **Keep a notebook.** Every time I find a great idea or think up something fun—a dancing horse or the like—I draw it in my notebook. Did your grandchild say something funny to you today? Write it in your notebook. Did you see a great star pattern on the dress of the person in front of you at the grocery store? Draw it out when you get to your car. Heard a good saying at church? Write it down. Did you doodle a little flower that is fun? Add it to your notebook. Then later, when you are tired and need a lift, take out your notebook (or in my case, notebooks) and "feed" yourself lovely drawings and thoughts.

7 Learn a new technique. Taking new classes and workshops help you grow as a quilter. Sometimes the smallest new thing can help you create wonderful new projects and send you on your way to new creative journeys. It's good to be adventurous to change direction once in awhile. Keep the mystery, excitement, and discovery in your quilting.

8 Let yourself laugh out loud! Be amused and happy. Life has enough things to bring out our serious side out. It's easier to create when we're happy and smiling, than when we're sad. Want to be a people-magnet? Be a happy, smiling, and enthusiastic person. Perhaps that's part of the charm of the children we love so much. Smiles come so easily to their faces.

9 Dream, dream, dream. My father is a big dreamer and always has been. My brother and I are both very good at using our imaginations, and many people have asked the question, "How do you think of these things?" Well, I have thought about that question a lot lately, wondering to myself, "Why don't people think of these whimsical things as easily as I do?" I think I learned to be creative because I was allowed to be a dreamer. As children, we played with our imaginations. We didn't need fancy toys. Dishpans, old scarves, empty cans, a ball of string, or bed sheets were our props for make-believe. We were always imagining our trips with pirates, or dances with Spanish dancers, or life in Africa, or the Black Forest, or dozens of other destinations. No idea seemed odd or silly as we were given permission to pretend. I have given this same permission to my children. In my workshops, as a student, you get a high grade for using your imagination. No idea is too far out there.

10 Buy a new book. Make your creative muscles grow. We have choices about the kinds of things we fill our lives with from day to day. By purchasing new books now and again, we are teaching ourselves new ways to stretch as quilters.

11 Get up and walk around. Most artists know that working on a project can make you tense up if you don't loosen those muscles. In art classes that I took, the teacher encouraged students to paint for awhile and then get up and stretch, drink a glass of water, look out the window, and just take a breather. Getting your blood flowing again can give you new eyes and attitude toward your art.

12 Start more than one project. Now, promise yourself that you will spend time with each and see them through to completion. I have about ten quilts going at any one time. I do not make myself any unreal time restraints as far as finishing them. I start different quilts to make myself change gears with color and style. If I am tired of one, or perhaps I am stuck on what to do next, I simply put it aside for another day and pick up a different project Your outlook and ideas change from day to day and this is what helps keep things going in a flow. What I might be stumped with today could be easily solved in a creative and unique way next week.

A SAMPLER FOR MY MOTHER 70" X 90"

Sometimes it is hard to make a quilt about someone you really love. My favorite saying to loved ones is, "I am going to make a quilt about you, don't plan on looking attractive." The nice thing is everyone has been honored to be remembered, so I am off the hook. They all still speak to me and understand the concept of folk-style quilts. So, this quilt is for and about my mother. My mother makes killer pies. I wanted to hand the recipe to my daughters, so I put the recipe in the center of the quilt. My mother's name is Geneva, and Dad calls her Ginnybug. My children call her Pom. I put in a teapot for her Canadian heritage (tea is important, after all). I included some of my Grandmother's orphan blocks, as well as old buttons from her button box. Behind the birds is my grandmother's old tablecloth, and the quilt is backed with four vintage tablecloths that belonged to our family. Putting in linens and textiles from your family makes your quilt more personal and special.

GOOD FAIRIES 43" X 49"

My children were always excited when they lost teeth. I was too, when I was young. I am hoping that this quilt will invite stories when I have my own grandchildren. My oldest daughter remembers one day when the tooth fairy left two cupcakes on the nightstand during naptime for her and her brother along with the money under the pillow. I wondered if she would notice that the same cupcakes were in the kitchen for dinner. She didn't.

TODAY I AM IN MY FORTIES 45" X 49"

I am sure most people who see this quilt wonder what in the world it means. The day before my fiftieth birthday, I had taught a workshop in Havre, Montana, and I had a sixteen-hour train ride home. I was in a playful mood (thank heavens), so I decided to do one more quilt while I was still in my forties. Two young girls across from me asked what my quilt said. I told them and explained it was my birthday the next day. One girl said, "I don't get it." "You will when you are forty-nine," I replied.

GOING NOWHERE FAST 51" X 56"

When I was small, we used to visit my grandparents' home in British Columbia. My grandfather had a big garden. Outside in the garden was a whirligig, which was a woman riding a bike. At night when the wind blew hard, you could hear the woman riding her bike really fast. I always remembered times in the garden and the woman, and thought it would be fun to put her into a quilt.

A BIT OF MARY LOU *46" X 53"*

I have taught a workshop for many years called "Five Easy Pieces." In this workshop we do our backgrounds and whatever tickles our fancy that day. I wanted a sample showing how you can include someone's name and then put in things they love. I made this little wallhanging for my studio wall. It usually travels a lot, so it hasn't made it onto the wall yet. But I do love the idea of the whimsy and the color.

Themes and Ideas

CRYSTAL LAKE MEMORIES 55" X 78"

In the Northwest, winters are beautiful and often white. One important memory for our family was a Thanksgiving visit with my Uncle Earl (Lovick) and Aunt Bonnie in Montana. Bonnie is a great cook, so Thanksgiving was always a treat, but the most memorable part of that trip was the day after. We got up early, made turkey sandwiches with the leftovers, and traveled to Crystal Lake and my uncle's cabin. Then we hiked to find our Christmas tree to bring back to Spokane. What fun it was choosing a special tree, laughing, watching the eagles fly high over the lake, the children making fake beards with tree moss, building snow men and snow forts, eating those delicious sandwiches, and celebrating time together with people we loved in the beautiful Montana wilderness.

20TH AND FREYA—A FIVE-YEAR-OLD'S VIEW OF HER MOTHER 64" X 49"

I remember vividly the backyard that we had when I was five years old. My mother had a large garden and she spent a lot of time in the backyard with my brother and me. I remember her talking to us and telling us lunch would be ready soon. When I got ready to do this quilt from memory, I couldn't remember what mom looked like, but then I remembered what I saw from a five-year-old's point of view. I get a lot of comments on this quilt, and my mother loves it.

HAPPY AUTUMN SAMPLER 56" X 48"

This quilt was a three-easy-pieces project. I took a theme, chose fabric that followed the theme, built a border, then filled in the background. A squirrel, acorns, and great leaves look super if you have a good color palette and varied scale with your prints

Themes and Ideas

Now that you have put on your thinking cap, here are
some suggestions for quilt ideas to celebrate:

Twinkling stars

Thanksgiving

Driver's License

Great report card

Sweet 16

Fourth of July

Favorite teacher

Good neighbor

Wonderful garden

First tooth

Graduation

Pride in your country

New Kitty

New dog

Happy birthday

Kwanzaa

First apartment

A cake baked by a child or with a child

Sharing conversation with a friend

Banana Split day

New shoes

Celebrating laughter

Spring cleaning

Remembering a loved one for so many things

Memorial Day

Election day

First day of school

Trip to anywhere

Happy finished quilt

Every day is a celebration

Getting well

Celebrating who you are

Celebrating someone who has helped you

Tooth Fairy

Pride in your church

New lipstick color

A day at the beach

First love

Sunshine is out

President's Day

Painting party

Wedding

Friendship

Voting
Flag Day
Picking fruit
Arbor Day
High tea
Barbecue
New car
Bowling
Badminton
Roller skating
Cookie swap
Ethnic dinner
Saint Patrick's Day
A visit to a circus
Ice cream social
New pen pal

Wildflowers

Delivering puppies
Playing cards, checkers, chess
Celebrating clean fresh sheets
Rummage sale or garage sale
Celebrating the smell of hot bread out of an oven
Celebrating your job or the people you work with
Celebrating a doctor, a nurse, a dentist
Celebrating time with yourself (your
best friend is you, after all)
Fresh tomatoes in your garden
Butterflies

First haircut

New House

Valentine's Day

Love your kids day

Welcome home

Shopping with a friend

Salary increase

Moving to new town

Bon Voyage

Ice Skating

Golf

Bar or bat mitzvah

Promotion

Father's Day

Skiing

Croquet

New baby

Celebrating rain on the roof top

Love your parents day

National quilt day

New Fabric

First dinner party

Nutcracker ballet

Adoption Day

Making a new friend

Grandparent's Day

Bowling

Celebrating healing

Baking cookies on a Saturday afternoon

Christmas

Children's Day

Love yourself day

Mother's Day

Love your friends day

Childhood

Engagement

Cooking

Opera

Summer is here

Spring is here

Winter is here

Fall is here

Moonlight

Rain

Now what can you think of celebrating that I haven't? There are hundreds of celebrations not listed here that are quilt stories waiting to be told about you, and the people and things you love.

Ocean breeze

 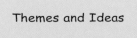

JASON AND JANELLE'S WEDDING QUILT 64" X 78"

I made this quilt for my son and daughter-in-law when they got married. I wanted the colors to be soft, I wanted it to be whimsical, and yet have names and dates. The wedding was a wonderful celebration for our family and I am glad that there is a quilt to remember it with. The buttons on the groom's shoes were the top tuxedo buttons worn by my husband and my son during the wedding. I tried to explain to my new daughter-in-law that anyone who had a quilt made about them was not going to be attractive and she would have to live with it. She laughed and was as good-natured as other family members have been. I guess she already has a good understanding of what folk art is.

EASTER TIMES REMEMBERED 70" X 58"

Easter has always been an important celebration time for our family. I remember my own egg-hunting days when I was small, and buying new hats every year with my mother as I grew older. My own children remember an egg hunt that my Aunt Bonnie and Uncle Earl in Libby, Montana, had for them one year. She provided a map with clues for Shari, my oldest child. As Shari read, the children ran through the house giggling and looking for more clues to the whereabouts of the hidden baskets. This remains one of my children's favorite memories. Mine too. Isn't it fun listening to children's laughter?

HOLIDAY HARRY AS SANTA 45" X 61"

I wanted to do something with a stack of fun-colored fabrics I had lying around. When the Holiday Harry idea popped into my head, I thought I would do a whimsical Santa to hang at Christmas. I cut out the Santa and decided he needed a supporting cast. Therefore I added the tree, a darling angel on top, Christmas balls for color, three stars in the sky for my three children, a moon, and some presents representing what gifts God has brought into my life—which is why Christmas is celebrated in the first place.

The nice thing about working on a book is that you give yourself the time to think about and research the theme or subject you are working on. Since the theme of this book is celebrations and seasons of life, I have surprised myself with the things I remember. At first I thought about holidays and gifts I had received. Then I started thinking about people and events.

I was surprised at how many picnics I remembered. Our family had so many wonderful picnics, and when I was in fifth grade, my parents bought a summer place. Fourth of July celebrations were so much fun! I also recalled that my brother and I bought orange slice candy, and sat on the banks of the lake. We watched as people walked into the water fully clothed during baptisms at the church camp next door. One day a week, we would go to the store, buy the candy, and watch as girls with beautiful white dresses and darling hair styles, and boys in white shirts with ties and black slacks would be submersed and then ushered back to shore to dry off.

Christmas memories are always fun to remember. But one of my most favorite memories is when my brother (a musician) and I went to visit an elderly neighbor from our childhood. This man was living in a nursing home, and when we went in to see him, he asked my brother to play the piano in the hospitality room. We walked down the hallway and passed many people slumped over sadly in wheelchairs or just sitting in the hallway. My brother walked up to the piano and started to play the most beautiful Christmas music, and one by one people wheeled in and surrounded the piano. It was like our own little Christmas miracle and I can hardly write this without being teary-eyed.

One year when my son was ill, he couldn't go out to visit Santa, and so we pooled our grocery money together and hired a store Santa to come to our home to visit. My three children were so excited that they were getting an early audience!

Snow brought adventure for me. I remember one year when the brakes on my brother's sled did not work. I went down a huge hill here in Spokane and slammed into a tree, breaking three fingers. It hurt, but everyone on the hill clapped wildly and said "Wow, cool!" I went back to school the next day, with a cast to show off, so it wasn't as bad as it could have been.

Speaking of brakes, at a St. Patrick's Day celebration my son borrowed a friend's bike and started riding down their steep driveway. No brakes then either, and he slammed into the neighbor's house across the street. Luckily, the lady was a nurse. I think we visited the emergency room five times that year with Jason. And each time he had broken something new. By the end of summer they knew us on a first-name basis.

Vacations were memory-makers for our family, too. One year we went to the Calgary Stampede, another year Mount Rushmore and Needle Mountain, and still another year horseback riding in Wyoming.

Rites of passage are always fun to remember. Like the time I dyed my hair and it turned green. Or the time I cut my doll's hair to prove to my mother that yes, it would grow back. It didn't. Or the time that I drove my dad's car forward into the freezer, then put it in reverse and took out part of the garage door. My boyfriend at the time said "Let me out of this car!"

My parents owned a large boat and I remember riding out to the middle of the lake, jumping in and trying to swim and dance to the music coming from the boat's stereo. At night we slept on board and listened to the water lap against the side. Boat owners did funny things too, like decorating their boats to match holidays. Wouldn't that make a fun quilt?

The point of these stories is that you have your own stories. Each event is an idea and a theme to begin your event quilt.

Getting Started

WELCOME HOME 48" X 55"

It was difficult when one by one my three children grew up and moved out. My husband and I love it when they come home for a visit. I had been thinking about how much fun it is when we are all together and wanted to make some kind of wallhanging for my entry wall that said "Welcome Home." As you can see, I did a folk-style couple and put three kids in the window of the house.

Backgrounds First

I started my design career doing paintings. My father and I shared an art room when I was growing up, and I learned from him, and later from my teachers in school.

Naturally, as a painter, I was used to having a canvas in front of me. I would fill in the background color and then go back and fill in the rest of the colors in my subjects.

This was what I found difficult about doing animals, people, and other things in quilts. There was no finished canvas, so I had trouble envisioning what the whole thing would look like. So, I came up with an idea to experiment and stretch my quilt making. I decided to make my background first, borders and all.

The first thing to do when making a background is to pile up many fabrics that look great together. Exercise a little abandon and let your color creativity have some fun. I use over twenty-five fabrics because I like scrappy quilts and colors that play well with each other. Then I dream up a block pattern I want to work with that day, simple or more complex. If I choose a nine-patch block, then I make many of them to carry around the background. My favorite size for a background is one yard of fabric. Then I cut a 1 1/2" to 2"- wide strip to frame the yard before I put my border on. This frames the center and announces, "This is the border." I then add my blocks to frame the entire piece.

Making the border first accomplishes two things. It lets you "see" the piece before you begin, and it gives you an invitation to stretch your creativity by allowing you to make choices about what you use in the center. I don't use blocks larger than eight inches so the border won't overpower my quilt.

Borders can be a series of strips, traditional pieced blocks, or more appliqué. I prefer pieced blocks because I think it is a nice balance with appliqué centers.

I think once you try this method of creating a quilt canvas, you will use it again. Making a quilt canvas makes perfect sense both for placement and design, and also for a terrific color recipe.

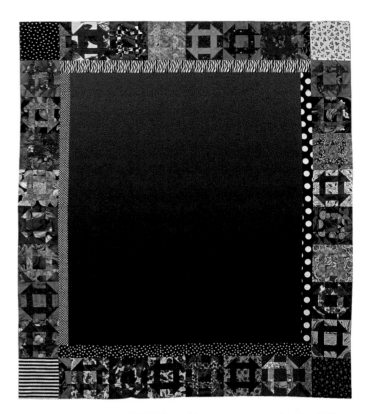

Fabric Styles and Color Recipes for Success

One of the first problems quilters have with color is how they look at a whole bolt of fabric and say, "That won't work, it's too bold." But what they don't realize is that once you cut a small 2" square or triangle, the large print they saw isn't what they will see in the quilt. Another frustrating thing is working with fabrics that are currently available. If you only buy fabrics you need as you are working on a project, you may not find the exact purple or red, green or blue you want. When I began to quilt, no one explained to me the importance of a fabric stash! My workroom is now so loaded down with fabric that I will never be able to use a fraction of what I have.

Last year my husband came down to my studio to ask me a question. He usually does not visit my sewing room unless he is changing the light bulb. As I was working on my computer, he looked at the three walls covered floor to ceiling with bookshelves that were crammed with fabrics of every imaginable color and design. I looked up from my computer just in time to see him with his hands on his hips as he exclaimed, "Holy smokes! You've gotta have a couple hundred dollars worth of fabric on those shelves!" Needless to say, I never take him fabric shopping with me, and after that comment, I never will. I am leaving well enough alone.

A PLAYFUL DAY IN THE GARDEN 52" X 61"

As I have said before, I love my garden. The neighbors' cats all love it too, because of the birds and squirrels and butterflies. So, one day when I was sitting outside with a glass of iced tea, I decided a little celebration of things in the garden would be a fun quilt to hang in my sunroom.

Falling into the Value Trap: Look Before You Leap

After I started traveling a lot and seeing more and more quilts and quilt shows, I noticed a huge problem that was rampant in the quilt world: many quilters do not understand the importance of value.

I have never seen your stash, but I bet you're like 90% of the quilters whose stashes I know. You buy mostly medium-value fabrics. That is, unless you love pastel baby quilts. If your stash is full of mediums, sometimes your quilts won't have the dramatic effect they could have. I tell my students to use a light-light background or a dark-dark background. Why? Because you want your beautiful medium fabrics to stand out, and you want viewers to see the story and things you have designed. This works with traditional quilts as well as story quilts. If you don't keep value in mind while working on a quilt, all of your story will moosh together, and you don't want that. Remember that a successful quilt often is credited with having sensational color, when in fact it is the value that sets it apart and makes it a prizewinner.

Color Wheel Recipes

The color wheel guarantees success if you know how to use it. The color wheel is easy to memorize and is well worth the effort. If you memorize the primary colors, the secondary colors, and each of their complements, you will know what goes with what any time you are shopping for fabric. You'll never have to second-guess yourself. Remember that a color loves its neighbors (on both sides) and it loves the people across the street, too (its complements). I use this color theory in the paintings I do and also in my quilts. If, for example, you decide that you love a purple fabric, you will notice its neighbors are blues and reds. I make a stack of these colors and then look across the color wheel to see what I might add for a complement and to make the quilt more interesting and striking. So, I might add swamp green. Green is a complement to red and any mixture of red, such as red-violet, red-orange, hot pink, etc. This is how I develop a recipe for a quilt before I ever start on the story. I also use many fabrics in the same color family and I tend to add other colors that I can get away with. My color confidence is the result of making hundreds and hundreds of quilts. It looks more scrappy and also appears that I have used many more colors.

If you aren't experimenting and having an occasional color flop, you aren't learning anything. I wouldn't be where I am today without giving myself permission to make mistakes and enjoy the process of learning and discovering.

I tell my students that I have four favorite recipes for color in quilts.

1 **Analogous.** Choose a fabric you love for its color, and then add neighboring colors. These quilts make beautiful quilts for any room in the house. See *Halloween Quilt,* page 83.

2 **Pick all primary colors**. Reds, blues, and yellows go together well and make for great drama and patriotic-theme quilts. See *Celebrating America Container Quilt,* page 45.

3 **Pick all secondary colors.** Oranges (peaches for a softer color), purples, and greens (teals are greens, remember). I personally think almost any greens work well together for variety and interest. Secondary colors used together make smashing quilts. See cover quilt.

4 **Choose one color in a fabric and then go straight across the color wheel to find its complement.** Then add a third color for variety. I like this method for a scrappy look. I use dozens and dozens of fabrics that all work with each other. Sometimes I use two complements in the same quilt, and if I am feeling really adventuresome, I use three colors and their complements. The trick here is to pull it together. This takes some work but is well worth it in the end. See *Holiday Harry As Santa* quilt, page 38.

Remember that the trick is to use lots and lots of scraps, but use them in the same color families for variety. The variety is what pulls you in and the color theme chosen keeps your attention because it looks good. Add value and you have a real winning quilt.

CELEBRATING AMERICA CONTAINER QUILT 48" X 56"

One of my most popular workshops is called "Container Quilts." In the workshop we design a container of any kind and fill it with things that are memorable, folksy, and fun. My friend Kathy gave me half a tablecloth after she took my class and used the other half. I went home and sewed it to a background and thus began an Americana theme. I love flags, watermelon, buttons, and I also do a fair amount of photo transfers in my things. So, I have my three children framed with great buttons, as well as fun flowers and a silly chicken. Notice the button I purchased in a Philadelphia antique shop. It reads "Be a Good Little Chicken." This has been fun to hang during the summer.

Fabric! "Krazy Kats and Mary Lou Too"

I am including examples of the fabric line I did for Benartex as an example of fabrics that I created to make a successful quilt. First of all you will notice the varied values, colors, and textures of fabric. This is what you want to keep in mind when you purchase fabrics for your own celebration quilts. You want to use a variety of scale in the prints. For example, sometimes my students have lots of small checkerboards in their stash. They have no dots, no theme prints, and nothing larger than a small check. They need to buy a larger print to add interest to their quilt surface. You want a variety of colors and scales.

I have also included many "light-giver" fabrics. This is my favorite style of fabric. Why? I choose light-givers because this style of fabric has lights, mediums, and darks painted onto the surface of the fabric. The eye will be drawn to that area that includes this fabric in your quilt.

Another important thing about these fabrics, is that they all work together colorwise. You won't have to guess about whether you can mix or match them. You can mix and match any of the fabrics and they will all blend in and look great. And even better, you can mix them in with your stash. See what great color and light-givers can do for your quilts.

So, when you go to the fabric store, remember value, scale of design, your color wheel, and remember light-givers. You will love the look of your quilts if you keep these simple elements in mind.

Appliqué

I want to say a word about the dreaded word "appliqué". Many quilters either announce "I don't do appliqué" or "I am a Baltimore Album quilter and I love appliqué." There are a lot of people in-between. How do I feel about appliqué? I don't worry about it. My stitches have become smaller as time goes on. They were bound to. I've made forty quilts a year for about five years. If my stitches show, I don't sweat it. If my thread does not match, I can live with that, also. I take projects with me on the road and often I have just one spool of thread in my purse. Do I worry if I am using black thread on a pink project? Naw. It's ok. And do you know why it's ok? It's ok because the whole point of these quilts is the story, the celebration, and not whether the thread matches. Do you think the members of your family care what color thread you use to tell their story? It is wonderful to have your work appreciated by your peers, but it is more important that the people who love you appreciate seeing Aunt Lucille holding the family recipe.

I appreciate fine workmanship and lovely quilting. I also appreciate quilt judges and I have quilt judges as good friends. But a story quilt should not take five years to make. The perfection should be in the story told and not in the technique or execution. Do I admire quilts with tiny, beautiful stitches that are masterpieces? Of course. And in fairness, I have seen quilts that should have had more time and care given to them. Hurrying and being sloppy isn't what I am talking about. But if you fear appliqué because someone judges your stitches, then you need to get over it and enjoy the product that you can design and execute.

CAN'T WE ALL JUST GET ALONG? 50" X 61"

Sometimes just a funny story can be a celebration when you remember it and laugh. My oldest daughter called from Calgary one day to say she was babysitting the neighbor's bird and prized fish tank. Since the neighbor was going to be in New Zealand for a good amount of time, this was a problem of sorts because my daughter owned three cats. We were due to visit with our dog, and I thought it would make a great subject for a quilt. We all laugh when we remember this story.

A LITTLE BASKET OF FOLK 18" X 29"

Container quilts come in all sizes. This quilt started on an airplane with the whack of a pair of scissors. I kept it small to make it manageable. That seemed important to me, since I had sewn a quilt to my dress the week before on a four-hour plane flight which was a real mess to rip out. Anyway, I used folksy-themed things and great embellishments and came up with this wallhanging that hangs in my kitchen.

Strips for Fun: Jots and Dots

ZIPPEDY DO DOG 47" X 54"

I have been having fun in workshops with this technique. I am including it in this book as an invitation to creativity. If you take some time and make some of these strips, you will find that you can make many unique and original quilts. I have started teaching a workshop based on this called "Jots and Dots," the jots being the strips and the dots being circles and rounded shapes. I have included this wall hanging called "Zippedy Do Dog" that I did, using this method, as well as some drawings of the shapes used.

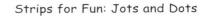

Below are the steps for making strips or jots.

1 Rotary cut 1"- up to 3"-wide strips from any yardage. Cut these strips on the straight of the grain, not on the bias.

2 Place a bowl of water mixed with a tiny bit of liquid starch by your ironing board. A good ratio to use is 1 cup of water to 1 $\frac{1}{2}$ tablespoons of liquid starch.

3 Take a piece of Teflon™ (silver) ironing board material and double it over once to provide a shield for your ironing board cover. You do this because otherwise you would burn a hole in your cover, which you do not want to do. Note: I go to a fabric shop and purchase one yard of 45"- wide ironing board cover fabric. This provides enough yardage to double over once and pin down on both sides to protect my ironing board cover.

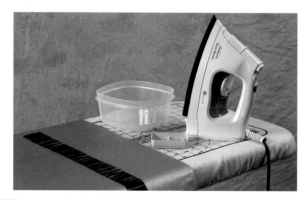

4 Dip your strip into the bowl of starch water. Run the strip between your fingers to wipe off excess liquid.

5 Place the tip of a pin into the ironing board protector fabric to lodge it.

6 Fold both edges of width of strip into each other wrong sides together.

7 With folded side down on the ironing board, slip the end under the pin, and pin the head of the pin over the open edge of the strip. This will serve as your guide as you press.

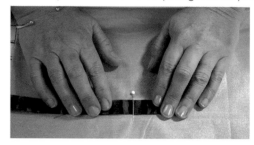

8 Now, you will need both hands to pull and guide the strip. Pull enough of the strip through to have the iron lay on the edge of the strip as it is pulled through the pin guide. Your right hand will pull the strip and your left hand will guide the strip so it keeps the fold centered. Your hand will not be touching the iron, as the iron will be laying across the strip to crease the fold.

9 Now take the strip, which will still be a little damp, and place it over a chair back or a drying rack to settle.

10 Try to put your next pin into a cool spot on your ironing board protector. This will prevent any holes from appearing due to heat.

I make many of these strips ahead of time in varied colors and widths. They are so much fun to have on hand for projects. They make great tree limbs, sun rays, legs for animals, fences. Use your imagination!

The strips can also be used to make letters.

1 Fold prepared strips into desired angles by creating tucks.

2 Pin or baste to quilt top and appliqué or top stitch in place.

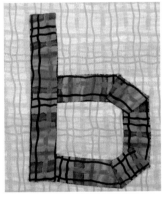
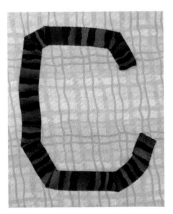

3 The top of the letter A is folded twice to create a blunt top.

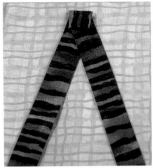

4 Create other letters by folding tucks at desired angles.

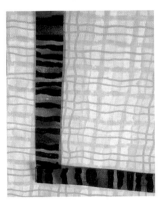
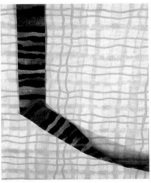
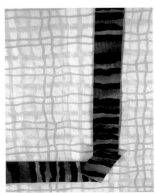

Buttons, Embellishments, Stuff:
Clean Out Those Cupboards, Drawers and Trunks

SNOW GRAMMA LIKE OURS 48" X 58"

Aren't grandmothers wonderful people? And isn't it great being a grandmother (for those of you lucky enough to experience it)? I really loved my grandmothers, and I thought that it would be fun to do a play on words using a snow gramma. I included five little snowmen on her representing, once more, our family. Pam Clarke made this even more whimsical when she quilted in snowflakes, words, and whimsy.

56   Quilted Memories

As I started thinking of celebrations and members of my family whom I celebrate with and about, I started thinking about all of the things in boxes in my drawers. Think of all the things you own that are sitting around gathering dust. This is a fun time to get creative with pieces of history, that were owned by someone special to you.

Consider your grandmother's buttons, old lace collar, handmade tea towels. Grandpa's lodge pin and things of this nature might end up at the nearest rummage sale. What might happen after you pass on and your relatives comment, "Let's get rid of this junk in mom's drawer, she hung on to any old thing?" If you include your treasures in a quilt, they are sure to be preserved in a better way than in a box. Likewise with old linens, vintage curtains, bark cloth, hankies and gloves worn by someone dear to you—see *A Sampler for My Mother,* page 24. I incorporated my grandmother's old tablecloth into the quilt. Remember how our aunts and grandmothers cut buttons, cuffs and collars off dresses to be saved and used again. What about little mementos picked up on vacations or trips that are small enough to be sewn to the surface of a quilt?

I admit that I am addicted to embellishments and buttons. I travel a good deal, and while I travel I am on the lookout for things that could be sewn on a quilt. Buttons are my first and most favorite passion. Black buttons become noses and eyes on snowmen. Red, purple and yellow buttons become flowers. Shapes and sizes used in combination can become outlines, rays of the sun, hair on dolls or animals. Buttons provide charm, texture, whimsy, and interest. Buttons make great eyeballs and gumballs. The good news is that there are wonderful button designers that create with you, the quilter, in mind. Buttons can make your quilt stand out. Buttons invite play and create style unlike anything else—see *Good Fairies* on page 25.

A note about sewing on buttons: I wait until the quilt is completed to sew on any treasures. I sew through all three layers of the quilt and use buttonhole twist or another heavy type of thread. You don't want to risk losing your buttons, so good thread and a little extra effort ensure they'll be there for many years to come.

Cake

As I have said before, I like taking a simple idea and expanding on YOUR creativity. Cakes are a very exciting and fun concept. Think of the times in your life when a cake was presented or eaten to celebrate a special day or occasion. Cakes come in all sizes and are made for all reasons. Think of different colors of cakes, designs on cakes, sizes of cakes; what about cupcakes, and three, four, or five-tiered cakes? What about things that sit on a cake or come out of a cake? What about candles, roses, or fancy icings, or animals on the cake? Who might be holding a cake or blowing out the candles of a cake? Who bakes cakes that is important to you? Is there a family recipe that could be included in a quilt for posterity? What about a special seasonal cake? Warm weather cakes might be different from cold weather cakes, and holiday cakes might have different colors and figures worked into the theme. Imagination is key here, and everyone has a great imagination if they take the time to tap into it. Give yourself a little time, and a notepad and pencil to write down cake related ideas.

I remember a summer vacation to South Dakota when all of the aunts, uncles, and cousins were gathered, and my Aunt Bess announced we were going to have a "Happy Unbirthday" party. She had bought simple little whimsical gifts, wrapped them up, and baked the largest, most elaborate cake you could imagine. There were a good number of relatives there, and we all sang "happy unbirthday to you" and laughed and cut the cake and opened gifts. That little bit of effort and creativity made a great memory for all of us.

If your memory is a bit rusty, ask a relative or friend what they remember that might be fun or charming or whimsical. Perhaps you would like to make a quilt cake to present to someone you love. Or make yourself a congratulations cake you wish you had received. Remember to be your own best cheerleader. How wonderful it would be to receive a cake wallhanging from someone that in effect says, "I appreciate you." It would surely make you and the person receiving it very happy.

Happy Birthday to you

Happy Fourth of July

Baby's Baptism

Bon Voyage

Wedding Cake

First Communion

Feel Better Cake

Bar Mitzvah

First birthday, 50th, 60th, 70th, 80th, 90th, 100 years old!

Happy Valentine's Day (hearts on cake or heart-shaped cake)

Happy anniversary—don't forget 1st, 25th (silver) and 50th (gold)

Congratulations on retirement Happy Graduation

Bat Mitzvah Welcome to the neighborhood

First touchdown, home run, stolen base, first goal, great basket, anything sports

Groom's Cake Congratulations on your new job

Congratulations on your promotion Christmas fruitcake

Celebrating with Crazy, Crazy Quilts

I have long been a fan of crazy quilts. You will notice that I have used whimsical, folk-style figures on my Crazy Quilt blocks. I like these crazy-style quilts because like my other quilts, you build your background first. I also allow myself to go outside the lines. If your figure is encroaching on another piece of the block, that's great. I let a lot of my pieces go visiting.

If you are wondering how to build a Crazy Quilt block, cut a chunk of fabric with five sides and begin building with new pieces of fabric in the same way you would a Log Cabin. Start in one side of the center piece, sew a chunk down right sides together, open and press, and then sew on the next piece. I make a group of squares (I like 12") and then I sew all the squares together before I start to appliqué. Once the top is together, pick a theme (as I did with the leaves of fall) and have some fun.

CRAZY FOR SUMMER 58" X 59"

I have always liked the concept of Crazy Quilts but have wanted to do them folk-style. I thought this book would present a perfect opportunity for you to pick a celebration theme of any kind and do a crazy, folksy, whimsical crazy quilt. I have done just that with this summer quilt. I took colors that are soft, and had fun designing things that remind me of the joys of summer. I then went to my embellishment pile and loaded it down with buttons, pins, and sequins that meant something or just looked good. Pam Clarke quilted many wonderful details such as names, dates and curlicues. This quilt looks smashing hanging up for guests to ponder and they spend a lot of time studying the details and fun secrets that are waiting to be discovered.

The Projects

General Guidelines

Instructions for the patterns shown in the book are going to be rather loose because I want to encourage your individual creativity. Please note the things that you need to keep in mind when beginning one of the projects.

Size

Each of the main patterns is offered at a small size, I encourage you to select a size you are comfortable working with. I usually make large wallhangings, and my preferred background size is one yard of fabric. The borders are always added to this yard of fabric. I prefer large wall hangings because they make a statement, and the turns and curves of larger pieces are easier to manipulate.

If you are like many quilters, you prefer a smaller wallhanging for a room or a small wall. Take your chosen pattern to your local copy shop, show them the permission to copy at the front of the book, and ask them to make a copy at the size you desire. I use the copy as my master pattern and trace it onto freezer paper. I then cut the pieces apart on the lines and iron them to the right side of my fabrics. I cut the pieces using a $1/4$" seam allowance. Then I clip almost to the paper all the way around each piece. Once I remove the paper, the clips remind where to turn under the fabric before I appliqué. I have used this method for years.

Once my freezer paper has been removed, I lay and baste the pieces onto the background using large stitches. This way I can "see" my celebration or memory as it will appear when it is sewn down. This gives me an opportunity to change my mind if a fabric does not work well. Then I begin sewing the bottom pieces down first, often clipping basting threads as I go along.

I use #10 needles and pull my all-cotton thread through folded fabric dryer sheets which makes my sewing bag smell good as well as keeping my thread fairly knot-free. I prefer this to wax.

Fabric Amounts: Yardages

 Because you are choosing the size of your quilt project, I do not have yardage amounts here. But if you notice, I like scrappy quilts. Most of my quilts have a 1 yard piece for the background. In addition to the background, I purchase many 1/4 yard and 1/3 yard cuts. Then I pick and choose from my large scrap pile. I like many fabrics in a small number of color categories. I suggest choosing a few colors and buying many fabrics with varied values in these colors. This makes your quilt interesting and also adds variety without being so wild that you lose the story of the celebration or the season.

Remember that this is your palette, just as an artist has a paint palette. If you don't have much variety in the fabrics you use, your quilt will not be as exciting as it could be.

For borders I often combine 1 yard of something plain, like a tone-on-tone or a solid black, with many scraps of varied fabrics. Value is important to remember in borders as well. If you follow these tips, you are sure to have a successful quilt.

Basic Pattern Instructions

1 Decide size for pattern and enlarge to desired size using a photocopy machine.

2 Choose fabric for background, border, and pattern pieces.

3 Construct background and add border of your choice.

4 Trace master pattern onto paper side of freezer paper.

5 Cut apart on lines of pattern pieces.

6 Iron freezer paper pattern pieces to RIGHT side of fabric.

7 Cut 1/4" seam allowance around all pattern pieces.

8 Clip around all pattern pieces just a scant short of freezer paper edge.

9 Remove freezer paper.

10 Lay out pieces on background.

11 Baste all pieces in place.

12 Appliqué beginning with bottom pieces first and top pieces last. Follow numbered appliqué order on pattern.

13 Once the pieces are appliquéd down, layer the wallhanging with low-loft batting and backing. Quilt as desired by hand or machine.

14 Sew on added details and embellishments.

Happy Birthday! Cake

30" x 50"

This quilt is a fun project. I designed a quilt with joy, color, and fun for you to make for someone you love. This quilt seems just the right thing for all of the above. I drew this out on a napkin when I was vacationing with my friends Sally Frey and Tonye Phillips in Gig Harbor, Washington. Sally wanted some kind of pattern to make up into a penny rug. Taking my drawing on the napkin, she made a darling penny rug (her specialty). I then decided it would make a great pattern for the book and would be fun made with all of my new Benartex fabrics, too. So, here you have two different ways to approach this joyful quilt. Wouldn't this make a wonderful gift for someone you love or a quilter who is close to you? It is a fairly fast pattern and you'll love giving it or keeping it around for those birthday parties you have for loved ones.

Holiday Harry Penny Rug, 24" x 17", made by Sally Frey

Quilted Memories

Candles and Flames Last

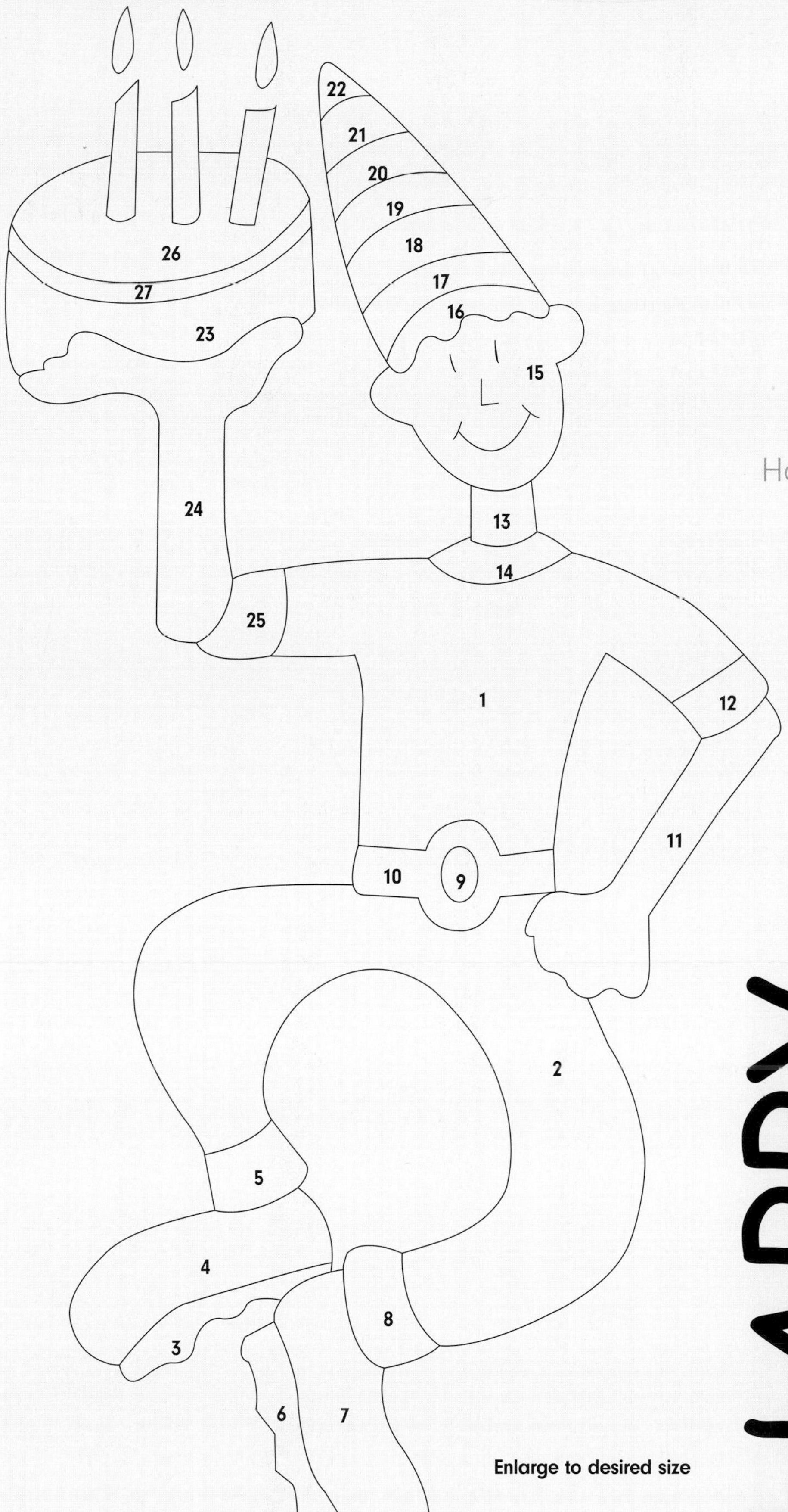

Happy Birthday! Cake

22
21
20
19
18
17
16
26
27
23
15
24
13
14
25
1
12
11
10 9
2
5
4
8
3
6 7

Enlarge to desired size

HAPPY BIRTHDAY

Sweet Treat Cupcake

14" x 17"

I wanted to make a little pattern that is simple and effective in saying you care about someone. This cupcake fits the bill if you are trying to think of a quick project. You can make it plain or add a name and birth date with a little embroidery to make it extra-special. Another thought is to have people in your small quilting groups all do a cupcake to create a wallhanging that has your names embroidered for a keepsake. These are fast and really work to let someone know you care.

Quilted Memories

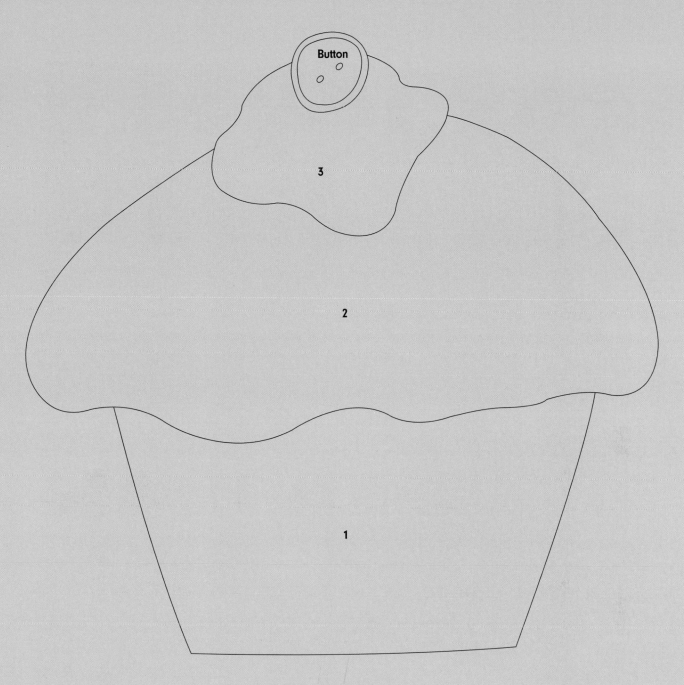

Button

3

2

1

Enlarge to desired size

Sweet Treat Cupcake

44" x 58"

A number of years ago, I got the idea to make an Uncle Sam who suggested that everyone quilt. I thought this would make an excellent pattern, as many quilters have said they would love this in their sewing room. I redesigned my original and came up with this super wallhanging. Wouldn't this be dandy in your sewing space or perhaps the family room or maybe entry hall? You could also have some fun with buttons that have an Americana flair as well. This quilt is sure to bring smiles, no matter where you hang it.

Enlarge to desired size

I Want You to Quilt

TO QUILT

I Want YOU

Shhh (Baby is Asleep)

6" x 12"

Since I decided to do a couple of small word-themed things for the book, I thought a little pillow might be in order. If you want to make a wallhanging instead, it would be good to hang on a doorknob or next to the door of a baby's room. I used soft colored fabrics with an infant in mind. This would make a good little tuck-in gift for a baby shower, also (no pattern given).

I Love You Dearly

12" x 18"

 Words on wallhangings can express so much. I chose these words to give to people in my life whom I do love dearly. Isn't it a nice thing to know how pleased and touched someone would be to get a little wallhanging that says "I love you dearly"? This would make a nice piece to hang in a bedroom, by a bed, as a reminder that you are loved.

Enlarge to desired size

Super!

13" x 15"

When my kids were in school I often wrote them notes and sometimes made a little poster out of paper. I have been thinking about that lately and wished I had thought of doing a nice little quilt for their door or room. This would make a wonderful surprise to some child coming home from school if it was hanging on his or her bedroom door. The reason? It could be as simple as remembering to feed the cat, a home run, a kind deed, a good grade, or an effort that calls for a simple reward. Or, how about just making it say "I think you are super." Remember, being a cheerleader can be rewarding and a lot of fun.

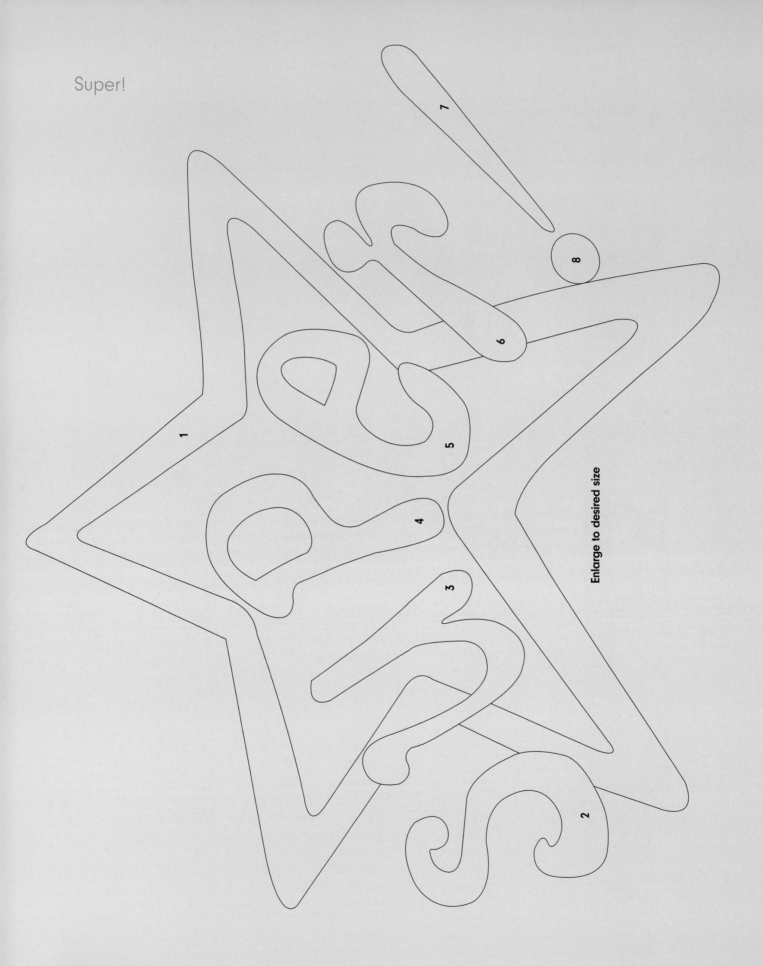

Enlarge to desired size

A Cake for Any Occasion

25" x 32"

This pattern was created for you to celebrate any event with the people you love. You can make this as it is in the photo, or add names, dates, and places to personalize it. This could become a real keepsake for someone. Perhaps you might choose to do a larger cake and put it out every year for a special occasion you celebrate with loved ones. There are so many reasons for celebrating with cakes, you have lots of avenues to use your own creativity. Have fun and spread smiles with others. This cake pattern is an easy way to achieve success in the happiness arena.

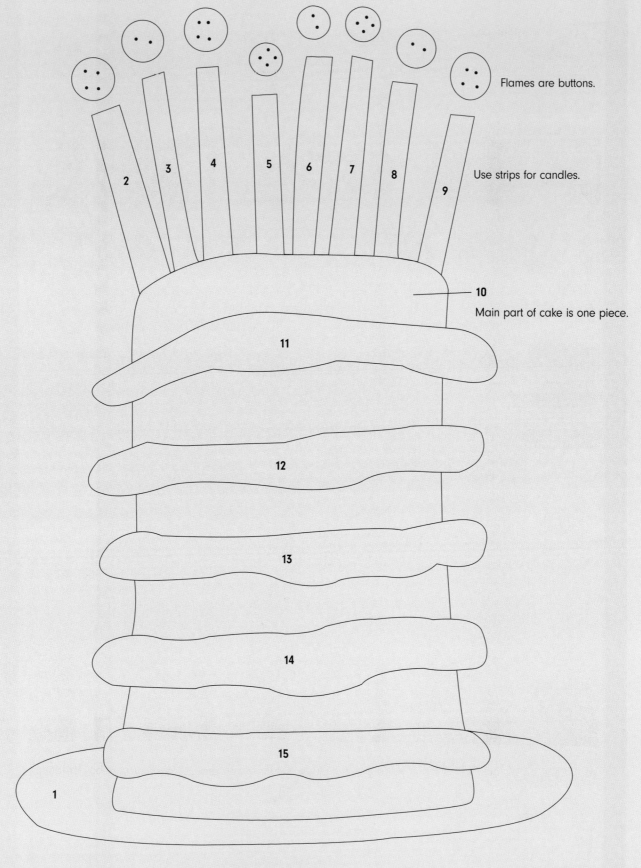

Flames are buttons.

Use strips for candles.

Main part of cake is one piece.

Enlarge to desired size

Fruit Cake

55" x 63"

I started this quilt with a ready-made background that my friend Naomi put together from border fabrics I stacked for her. All of the border blocks contain fruit-themed fabrics. I let the background sit around for a while so I could think about what I wanted to appliqué onto the center. I had been thinking about doing a girl coming out of a cake for years. So, I took my pencil and sketched out a darling girl who was part of a cake. It made perfect sense to me and it provided a pattern to make for someone very special. I topped the quilt off with my favorite fruit, cherries. If you wanted to be more creative, you could do lots of different fruits on the cake, or animals on the cake, or toys. There is no end to the themes you could stretch with on this project. How about someone's name in letters? This would make a terrific gift. Pam's quilting added a smashing effect.

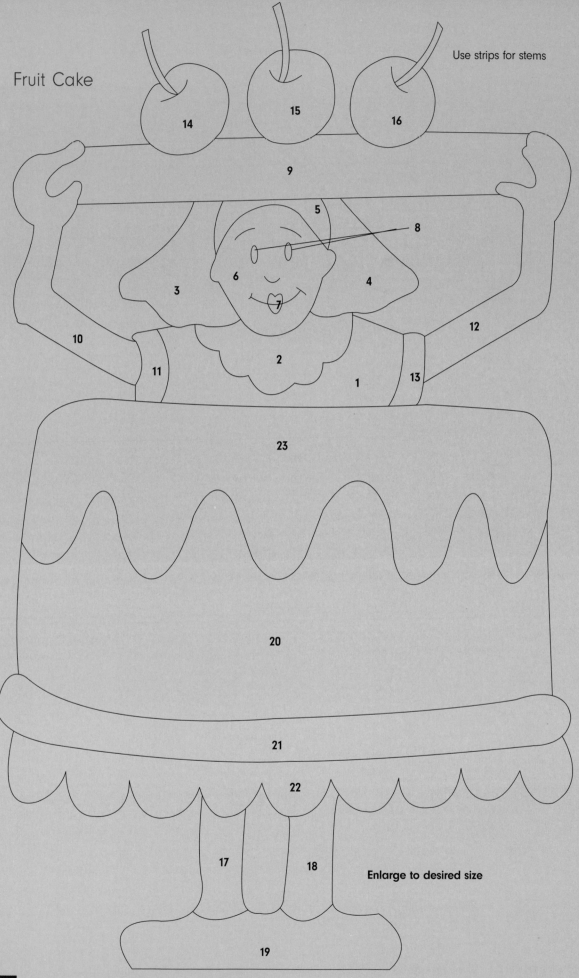

Fruit Cake

Use strips for stems

Enlarge to desired size

40" x 50"

I will become a grandmother in October, 2001. With that in mind, I started designing a quilt for my future grandchildren. I designed a stork years ago and thought he would be keen in a cabbage patch. So, as you can see here is Sammy Stork picking up his next baby to deliver to some lucky parents.

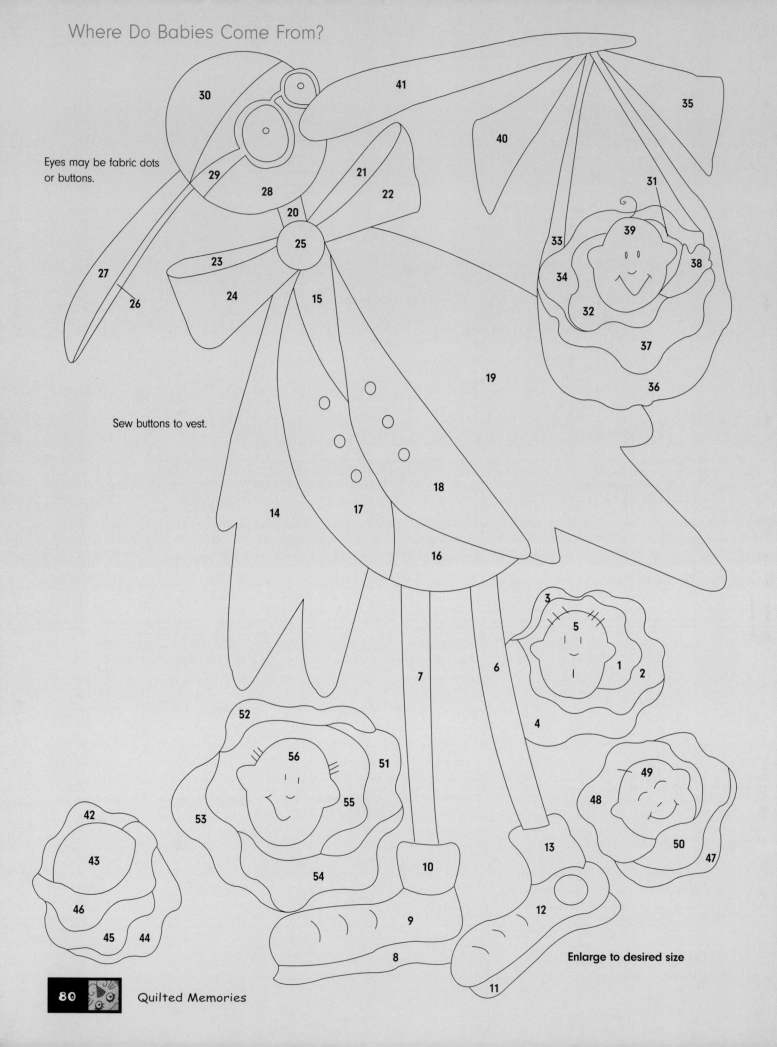

Eyes may be fabric dots or buttons.

Sew buttons to vest.

Enlarge to desired size

Holiday Harry Quilt Gallery

I like challenges, and had been thinking about a challenge that would be fun and interesting. The challenge was to take a fun character and create a celebration quilt using Harry or his wife Mayzie. I had such a large response, I could not include all of the quilts in this book.

MOM LOVES HATS

BY JEANNE N. MILLS OF PACIFIC GROVE, CALIFORNIA, 32" X 42"

This quilt was made to record my 86-year-old mother's fondness for buying and wearing hats. When I vacationed with her recently and watched her purchase four hats in three days, I realized I had a story to tell and a warm memory to record in fabric. I love appliqué, so what fun to have a large surface to hand stitch. My mom was thrilled: "Did you make this quilt for me?" I loved seeing her excitement, and "joie de vivre."

HALLOWEEN QUILT
BY HEATHER ANNE POOL OF PORTLAND, OREGON, 68" X 66"

I love the excitement of autumn. Leaves whipped up by the wind, big yellow moon, dressing up, trick or treating through the neighborhood after dark, candlelit jack-o'-lanterns and the thrill of all that candy! My Halloween witch is trying to sweep up, but the wind may be getting the better of her. The poem stenciled on the quilt is by Hambert Wolfe.

VISIONS OF HANUKKAH
BY VICTORIA JACOBS, ©2000, AND TERRI LANNING OF SACRAMENTO, CALIFORNIA, 33" X 39"

Holiday Harry has visions of Hanukkah dancing in his head. In his dreams he sees his children playing the dreidel game, his mother is serving latkes, the Menorah is lit and there are gifts for the children. This quilt incorporates all of the things that make Hanukkah such a special celebration.

THE BOYS ON HOLIDAY
BY SUSAN S. WETZSTEON OF HAMILTON, MONTANA, 56" X 56"
This quilt was made in honor of our sons' birthdays, which are one day apart from exactly two years difference. For the past few years we've gone to Sun Valley in June for their birthday weekend. They spend their time doing what they love best, golfing, mountain bike riding, and fishing. Cory, the oldest, is golfing and in the green. I quilted his name, birthday, and golfing terms. Andy is on the bike and the mountain is quilted with his name, birthday, and biking terms. The quilt is hand appliquéd and hand quilted.

EVERY DAY IS A HOLIDAY WHEN YOU'RE RETIRED
BY JAMIE GRANT OF HAMILTON, MONTANA, 72" X 72"
This was inspired by my folks and the fact that they celebrated their 50th wedding anniversary this year. They live on Flathead Lake, and grow cherries and make wine for fun! The title of the quilt is what my dad always says about retirement. I did some surface quilting and then hand appliquéd the picture on top. I have done a number of smaller quilts and really like the way this looks.

NAKED LADIES
BY MARY ELLEN PARSONS , ©1997, OF CARMEL VALLEY, CALIFORNIA, 31" X 38"
Each year in our area of California, I eagerly await the appearance of the "naked ladies," glorious pink flowers on bare stems without leaves. They are also known as Belladonna lily, a member of the Amaryllis family, and appear as if by magic in late summer or early autumn. When dry summer has turned our region to golden brown, this burst of color is truly a cause for celebration. This quilt cloaks the real need to celebrate and nurture an important resource for quiltmakers. It is a resource filled with wonderful fabrics, supplies, and inspiration—our neighbors, the local quilt shops.

FORE! CHARLIE
BY PAT BISHOP OF CASTRO VALLEY, CALIFORNIA, 54" X 56"

My husband Charlie has made golf his life. He has played from Florida—with a pet alligator named Charlie on the course—to California with many deer, and loved it all. The three flags denote a hole-in-one on the number indicated. Charlie is a marshal on his home course and has volunteered at several amateur and professional tournaments, such as the U.S. Open in Monterey. When he is happy, I am happy—quilting, of course.

COOKING UP ADVENTURE
BY SUSAN MCDERMOTT OF LOMPOC, CALIFORNIA, 53 ½" X 60"

When Mary Lou issued the challenge, I thought of Harry as a Santa, an Easter bunny, a leprechaun, or a very interesting president. But my Harry had ideas of his own. Tired of the traditional and predictable, Harry packed his bags, left the rat-race far behind and boarded a flight of fancy. Envisioning himself with lots of interesting settings, he finally landed, sunscreen in hand, on a faraway beach. He is now "Cooking Up Adventure" in the warm sunshine amidst island critters. There he will stay until he hops aboard a steamer and sails to the next exotic port of call. While gazing at his vacation pot of soup, let your imagination take your own flight of fancy. Bon voyage!

RETIRED!
BY RUBERTA COOPER PETERSON OF CULVER CITY, CALIFORNIA, 48" X 52"

Cats are great fun to work into quilts. You can make them silly, serious, crazy, and loveable, or anything else you can think of. But then, that's the way they are in real life, too. This quilt was made with my twenty-two year old grandson in mind. He is an avid fisherman, and constantly talks about his plan to retire at age fifty.

THEY DISAPPROVED OF THE WEARABLE ART PEOPLE
BY WILDA NORTHROP OF PACIFIC GROVE, CALIFORNIA, 40" X 60"

When the San Jose Quilt Museum put out a call for humorous quilts, I was eager to participate because I am always trying to laugh in other parts of my life—and why not quilting? The postures and overall style of the women in this quilt were inspired by artist Erika Oiler, who designs a line of greeting cards, as well as other art. It was an opportunity to celebrate the ability to laugh at ourselves. This verse accompanies the quilt:

Erika Oiler, card artist divine,
Gave the women their look, the story is mine.
Madge whispered her bias, filled with disdain,
Hating their style, she thought them insane.
She talked to her group, convinced them of that,
And there they all so indignantly sat.
Bigotry's wrong and so is the vest.
Everyone's funny however they're dressed.
By Wilda Northrop

BEACH HOLIDAY
BY SHELBY DIEHL OF COTO DE CAZA, CALIFORNIA, 50 ½" X 53 ¾"

I didn't know such a fun and whimsical-style quilt was hiding in my head until I took a workshop from Mary Lou. "Just put the pencil to the paper and start", she said. So I did, and it turned out to be one of the most fun and rewarding quilts I have ever made. "Beach Holiday" was inspired by my summer vacations to the quaint island of Ocean Isle in North Carolina. One of my favorite things is the colorful beach umbrellas lining the shore. There is an art and routine to putting (and keeping) them up. Like regular umbrellas, they turn inside out and can blow away, and their size makes this quite a sight!

HAPPENING HARRY
BY JULIE M. LYNCH AND CASEY J. LYNCH (DESIGN) OF GREENACRES, WASHINGTON, 45" X 51"

When Mary Lou approached me about creating a Holiday Harry, I resisted. But with time for thought and my resident artist Casey, I decided my Harry should go for broke, celebrating many holidays at once. My son Casey drew Harry with style and class! Thank you, Mary Lou, for the challenge, and thanks to Casey for all the talent he freely shares.

HOLLY DAY WALKS HER DOG
BY SUSAN FLEMMING ENGEL OF VICTOR,
MONTANA, 55" X 64 1/2"

The idea of being able to use a "play on words" in the Holiday Harry challenge really appealed to my sense of silliness. Holly Day immediately popped into my head and then her holiday dogs got in the act. Thanks, Mary Lou, for encouraging free-hand cutting.

ROAMIN' HOLIDAY IN MONTANA
BY JERRY KELLEY OF BEAUMONT, TEXAS, 55 1/2" X 44 1/2"

This quilt was inspired by a visit by the Blockheads Quilting Bee from Beaumont, Texas to Montana. They traveled by private plane to the Flying Dog Ranch in Bozeman, Montana. Some of their activities represented on the quilt are a helicopter tour of the Gallatin Valley, a dinner party prepared by chef Hunter Lacey, a day of shopping in Jackson, Wyoming, a river-rafting trip, and of course lots of sewing and visits to three local quilt shops. Animals on the quilt are "Digger" the black lab and "Floyd", the cat who allows humans to share his home.

THE LAST STITCH
BY DEBRA HAIGH OF CAMARILLO,
CALIFORNIA, 48" X 60"

This is a depiction of quilting friends sharing that rare moment of pure celebration only quilters understand; The Last Stitch!

MR. WONDERWEAR
BY STASI MORRISON WILSON OF TEMECULA,
CALIFORNIA, 27 X 42 ¹/₂"

PRINCESS FANCY PANTS
BY STASI MORRISON WILSON OF TEMECULA,
CALIFORNIA, 27" X 42 ¹/₂"

In our family there is a great celebration when each child leaves the dependency on diapers and forges into the future with great confidence in their "big kid" pants. My son, Jared Count Wilson, was changed from a mild-mannered boy into "Mr. Wonderwear". Jared's cousin, who is three months younger, experienced a transformation of her own. She, Susanna Marie Elliott, was now the beautiful, high-stepping, tip-toeing "Princess Fancy Pants" she always knew she was inside.

BOXING DAY
BY DEB COLE OF BARRIE, ONTARIO,
CANADA, 30" X 47"

Santa and the elves stop at "Holiday Harry's Inn" after a brutal twenty-four hour Christmas run. A little R & R is just what they need before continuing on to the North Pole to start making next year's toys. Holiday Harry is decked out in the traditional "Hudson Bay"™" parka trimmed with mink and wearing his red leather mittens.

HARRY'S JULY 4TH
BY ELLENE GRAVELLE OF RIDGECREST, CALIFORNIA, 42" X 60"

A large stash of patriotic fabric was my inspiration for designing a Fourth of July Harry. Lighthouse, shorebirds, mollusks, whale watching, sand dunes, and fireworks are all elements of favorite family vacations of the past. The biggest interpretation challenge I had was creating the fireworks. With Mary Lou's encouragement, and application of her philosophy that there are no rules in folk art and anything goes—it happened.

HOLIDAY HAIRYED
BY TONYE PHILLIPS OF CAMP SHERMAN, OREGON, 45" X 50"

This Holiday Harry is definitely "hairyed." I had a blast collecting all of the different holiday fabrics for his hair. Harry looks like how many of us feel around the holidays. This Harry began to take shape as the Christmas holidays started to reach a fever pitch last year. Barely hanging on to his credit cards while tangled in the Christmas lights. Giving a lot of thought to this project, I was really searching for a play on words. They tickle my funny bone. Most of the quilts that I do have a vintage feel and look to them. So Holiday Harry was just what I needed to stretch. Before I realized what was happening I was actually becoming more comfortable designing my own quilts! Wow!

CATCH US IF YOU CAN
BY JACKIE SEIDELL OF WALNUT CREEK, CALIFORNIA, 46" X 52"

Baking is always a big part of my family's holiday traditions. Everyone always enjoys our cookies and especially my Mom's gingerbread men. I remembered an old European tale of the gingerbread boy who ran away from his maker, and decided to have the gingerbread boys flying out of the bowl. Sandi, our yellow lab, is always underfoot in the kitchen hoping for a treat, and thus needed to be part of the scene. This was my first completely original quilt and was a lot of fun to make.

HOLIDAY WISHES
BY DAWN TONIOLI OF ANAHEIM, CALIFORNIA, 54" X 51"

This quilt represents my daughter Debbie's ultimate Christmas list. She asked for a BMW convertible, diamond earrings, a part in the movie *Miracle on 34th Street*, a trip to Maui, a Movado™ watch, and a trip to Spain on a special invitation from Antonio Banderas. She is such a good daughter, that I threw in a new car FOR HER, too.

Conclusion

So, are you ready to begin? Are you inspired? I certainly hope so. This was my aim. Creative celebration quilts are the perfect vehicle to show us what you stand for and who you are.

I wrote this book to encourage you to stretch your ideas and more important, to give yourself permission to make unique quilts that celebrate. I am hoping that by reading this and seeing my quilts, you now have more ideas than you can believe. I also hope that you feel close enough to me by now that you will take my advice and make a number of quilts celebrating your life and the lives of those you love. I am hoping that someday someone will look at one of your quilts and be inspired after understanding who you are and what is vital and important to you. All you need to do is begin. So, give yourself permission, let go, fill out your brainstorm list, put together a great stack of fabrics you love and start creating that celebration quilt. By doing so, you will certainly put a little more joy in this world that needs more joy and more celebration.

In closing I leave you with my favorite reminder: Every end has a beginning.

About the Author

Mary Lou Weidman is from Spokane, Washington where she lives with her husband Mark. Mary Lou and Mark have three children: Shari, Jason and Shelbi. Shari and her husband Mark (Doc) live in Calgary, Alberta. Jason and his wife Janelle live in Spokane. Mary Lou has been interested in quilting since 1974 and folk art since the 1980s. She enjoys the people she meets teaching nationally and internationally. Mary Lou began designing fabric in 1997 and has authored other quilting books. Mary Lou and her husband are avid gardeners and enjoy their backyard when weather permits. Mary Lou's goal in life is to make all of the quilts she has stories for.

To contact Mary Lou about workshops or other questions:
MARY LOU WEIDMAN
9116 E. SPRAGUE #442
SPOKANE WASHINGTON 99206
LATTEGIRL@AOL.COM

Resources

Buttons

JUST ANOTHER BUTTON COMPANY
924 Wheat Ridge Dr.
Troy, Ill. 62294
This company does wonderful polymer clay sculpted buttons to add whimsy and color to your quilts. These buttons are washable. Many, many designs, all great! Found in your favorite quilt shops around the world.

THERESA'S HAND DYED BUTTONS-HILLCREEK DESIGNS
9518 Hillcreek Way
Santee, CA 92071
Theresa@hillcreekdesigns.com
This company serves up beautiful buttons that are hand dyed to match literally any fabric you are working with. I have personally sewn on thousands (I am not kidding). They are washable and look great on quilts and clothing. They are available in your favorite quilt shops.

GEDDES STUDIO
9472 Golden Drive
Orangevale, CA 95662
916-988-3355
www.geddesstudio.com
The woman who owns this does amazing work. These glass buttons are works of art In themselves and you will pick them out quickly in this book. You may find these in your local quilt or fashion fabric shop and if not, ask them to call Nancy with an order.

SUSAN CLARKE ORIGINALS
653 Jackson St.
Red Bluff, CA 96080
randy@tco.net
These metal and glass buttons are treasures in the shapes of bees, butterflies, bunnies, cherries and hundreds of other magical things, all hand painted. I put these liberally on my quilts in house windows, a woman's ring finger, a hat, a kitty collar and about any place your imagination can take you.
Available at your local quilt shop.

JHB BUTTONS
Found in your local quilt and fabric stores. Hundreds of wonderful designs just waiting for you to sew them to your favorite story quilt. These people have thought of every kind of button known to man.

Machine Quilting

Home Stitches/Pam Clarke
2710 W. 47th Ave., Spokane, WA 99224
509-747-0315
Pam has quilted each of my quilts for many years and has come up with the designs on her own, showing what an artist she can be. She also teaches workshops across the U.S. and Canada..

Index

Other Fine Books from C&T Publishing

Along the Garden Path: More Quilters and Their Gardens, Jean Wells and Valori Wells

The Art of Classic Quiltmaking, Harriet Hargrave and Sharyn Craig

Cut-Loose Quilts: Stack, Slice, Switch & Sew, Jan Mullen

Diane Phalen Quilts: 10 Projects to Celebrate the Seasons, Diane Phalen

Fantastic Fabric Folding: Innovative Quilting Projects, Rebecca Wat

Freddy's House: Brilliant Color in Quilts, Freddy Moran

Free Stuff for Quilters on the Internet, 3rd Ed. Judy Heim and Gloria Hansen

Free Stuff for Sewing Fanatics on the Internet, Judy Heim and Gloria Hansen

Free Stuff for Stitchers on the Internet, Judy Heim and Gloria Hansen

Free-Style Quilts: A "No Rules" Approach, Susan Carlson

Hand Appliqué with Alex Anderson: Seven Projects for Hand Appliqué, Alex Anderson

In the Nursery: Creative Quilts and Designer Touches, Jennifer Sampou & Carolyn Schmitz

Laurel Burch Quilts: Kindred Creatures, Laurel Burch

The Quilted Garden: Design & Make Nature-Inspired Quilts, Jane A. Sassaman

Quilting with the Muppets: The Jim Henson Company in Association with Sesame Workshop

Quilts for Guys: 15 Fun Projects For Your Favorite Fella

Start Quilting with Alex Anderson, 2nd Edition: Six Projects for First-Time Quilters, Alex Anderson

For more information write for a free catalog:
C&T Publishing, Inc.
P.O. Box 1456
Lafayette, CA 94549
(800) 284-1114
e-mail: ctinfo@ctpub.com
website: www.ctpub.com

For quilting supplies:
Cotton Patch Mail Order
3405 Hall Lane, Dept. CTB
Lafayette, CA 94549
(800) 835-4418
(925) 283-7883
e-mail: quiltusa@yahoo.com
website: www.quiltusa.com